RESUME RESULTS

by Brian Harris, B.A., M. Ed.

A step-by-step guide to help you write an amazing resume to get more job interviews and get hired into the job of your dreams.

ISBN 9781791612139

CGS COMMUNICATIONS, INC.
www.cgscommunications.com

TABLE OF CONTENTS

"Insanity is doing the same thing over and over again and expecting different results."
Rita Mae Brown

INTRODUCTION

Recently I worked with an unemployed man who had mailed out over 500 resumes with only one response. I told him that it was time to consider a new approach. If you have experienced some difficulties in getting hired into the job that you want, then it may be that you need a new approach as well. The purpose of an effective resume is to help you get an interview for the job you are applying for. Your resume (and cover letter) is your entry ticket to get your foot in the door to be considered for a job. If you are sending out resumes and not getting very many interviews, then it is very likely that your resume needs to be revised.

RESUME RESULTS can help you to create a professional looking resume with content that is based on the insider secrets of what employers are looking for. Based on my more than 20 years of counselling students and adults to obtain meaningful jobs, whether part-time or full-time, I believe the content of this book, if followed closely, can help you to have a more effective resume.

In this book I will share with you many proven tips that I have learned from helping people to be successful in applying for jobs. I will also share the results of my research with employers as I sought to better understand the most important factors employers look for when they hire new employees.

The first chapter in this book will review your understanding of what job is best for you. Knowing which career you are looking for is critical to your future success. It is very difficult to write an effective resume if you don't have a clear picture of the career that is best for you.

The second chapter can help you to better understand what employers are looking for when they hire new employees. For example, a successful advertisement addresses the needs of potential customers. As you watch advertisements on television or view them in magazines, consider the thousands of dollars that have been spent in preparing these advertisements. A critical aspect of designing any

The main purpose of your resume is to help you get a job interview.

Do you know what employers are looking for when they hire?

advertisement focuses on the needs of the customer. Similarly in looking for a job, it is important for you to understand what employers are looking for. When your cover letter, resume and job interview answers meet the needs of the employer, you will experience greater success. Based on my interviews with leaders from hundreds of companies I will share six insider tips that can help to make your resume stronger.

When your cover letter, resume and job interview answers meet the needs of the employer, you will experience greater success.

Chapter 3 will help you to identify your personal skills (your soft skills). There are generic personal skills that most employers are looking for. What are these skills and how can you present them on your resume to help you stand out from others who are applying for the same job? Personal skills include getting along with others, having a positive attitude, and being a self-starter (although there are other personal characteristics to also consider).

Chapter 4 will help you to identify the job-specific skills that are important to address in your resume. Every job requires a set of skills that is specific to that job. Understanding exactly what an employer is looking for in terms of job-specific skills can be very important to the success of your resume.

Chapter 5 will provide some tips on how to use keywords in your resume which can help you to stand out from other job applicants. In addition, many businesses have the technology to scan resumes to search for keywords that are important to that business. If you don't include the keywords in your resume that a business is looking for, your resume might never even get into the hands of a human.

Chapter 6 brings together your learning from the past three chapters to help you to decide what should actually be included on your resume. In this chapter you will learn how to use keywords to present your personal and job-specific skills to best meet the needs of the employer. Matching your skills to the needs of an employer is critical for resume success.

In Chapter 7 you will look at some potential layouts for resumes to help you to decide what is the best way to format your resume. You will be given some proven tips on how to set up your resume so that it will be more effective.

Chapter 8 will help you to prepare your resume for digital submission, whether you are sending your resume by email or whether you are expected to post it online. If your resume is going to be submitted digitally, how is the preparation of this resume going to be different than a resume you might print on a piece of paper? This chapter can help you to understand how to create a more effective digital resume.

In Chapter 9, you will have the opportunity to take all your learning so far in this book and create an amazing resume. This chapter will help you to create a strong resume using an easy-to-use step-by-step process.

Finally in Chapter 10, I will answer some of the questions you might have regarding some other aspects of your job application such as your cover letter and job interview.

*Taking your first
step in the right
direction
is more
important than
taking many steps
going
the wrong way.*

"All successful people have a goal.
No one can get anywhere unless
he knows where he wants to go
and what he wants to be or do."
Norman Vincent Peale

THE BEST CAREER FOR YOU

Before we take a look at anything to do with writing a resume, let's take a brief look at the job you are applying for. If the job that you are applying for doesn't build on your strengths, this might undermine the effectiveness of your resume before you even get started in writing one. When you apply for a job that matches your strengths, you will be more enthusiastic in all aspects of your job application, and employers will recognize this in a positive manner. When you apply for a job you don't really want or one that doesn't give you the opportunity to do the things you really enjoy doing, an employer will recognize your lack of passion or enthusiasm for the job. What I am really trying to say here is that one of the key factors in writing an effective resume is first of all choosing a job to apply for that creates some excitement in you. Applying for a job that you believe will be personally satisfying is an important first step in any job application.

In workplace research, the people that are the happiest in their jobs are those who are doing what they like to do. If you are applying for a new job (or even a first job), it makes sense to be applying for jobs, if at all possible, that will give you the opportunity to do things that you like to do. It has often been said that when you choose a job you love, you will never have to work a day in your life.

In his bestselling book *GO - Put Your Strengths to Work*, author Marcus Buckingham states:

> *"You will be most optimistic, most courageous, and most ambitious when playing to an area of strength. And when you hit resistance or obstacles to your goals, you will bounce back faster when those goals center on one or your strengths. Your strengths are your multiplier. Your strengths will magnify you."*

What are your strengths? What are the careers that best match your strengths? If you are uncertain of your answer to these questions you might find it useful to read my book *Choosing A Career* be-

"Success is achieved by developing our strengths, not by eliminating our weaknesses."
Marilyn vos Savant

fore completing this book (and for students, you might find it helpful to read my book *After High School*). Both *Choosing A Career* and *After High School* have self-scoring interest surveys in them that can help you to identify which careers are best for you.

> *"Find out what you like doing best, and get someone to pay you for doing it."*
> Katharine Whitehorn

Throughout this book, you will be asked to look at job advertisements. These advertisements can be very helpful to you as you develop an effective resume. It is strongly suggested that you take a small box, file folder, or a 8 1/2 X 11" envelope to store your job ads (let's simply call this your Job File). If you use the Internet to locate job advertisements, then it is recommended that you print some of the ads and place them in your Job File, or you could even set up a file folder on your computer, tablet, or cell phone to store your ads. You will find it very helpful that everyday when you are completing the activities in this book that you continue to find and place job advertisements in your Job File. Later chapters will ask you to refer to the job advertisements in your Job File as you receive step-by-step instructions for writing an effective resume.

> *"The future depends on what you do today."*
> Mahatma Gandhi

One of the most important ingredients for achieving success is taking action. A dream without action is still just a dream. To help you take action, there will be easy-to-use **ACTION STEPS** throughout this book that can help you to be successful in your job search.

ACTION STEP #1

Prepare a Job File. This can be a box, an envelope, or a folder on your computer. Every day as you continue in this book, add at least one job advertisement of a job that is of interest to you in your Job File.

You can find job advertisements in the classified section of local newspapers (whether as print of online sources) or through job sites such as:

www.indeed.com
www.careerbuilder.com
Google for Jobs

BOX 1

Tips On Finding Your Next Job

1. Research websites of companies that you think might hire people for the job that you are seeking.

2. Contact Human Resources Departments.

3. Talk to people who already work in the job you are seeking.

4. Have someone who works in a company you are interested in check their company staff room bulletin boards.

5. Research career related websites.

6. Check newspaper classified sections.

7. Use the telephone book to locate companies you might be interested in. Contact the companies to inquire where they advertise for new employees.

8. Read newspaper business sections for companies in the news who may be expanding their operations.

9. Use community career help services, employment agencies, and school guidance or placement services.

10. Locate trade publications and business directories. (often found in library reference departments)

11. Contact temporary job agencies.

12. Talk to friends, relatives, neighbors, teachers, coaches, etc.

13. Attend "Job Fairs".

14. If you are still in school, inquire whether you can pursue a co-op placement in your chosen field.

15. Talk to company owners about employment opportunities.

"The aim of marketing is to know and understand the customer so well the product or service fits him and sells itself."

Peter Drucker

WHAT ARE EMPLOYERS LOOKING FOR?

One of the keys to any successful marketing is understanding what the customer is looking for. In many ways, applying for a job is a form of marketing. The employer is your customer and you are attempting to market yourself to him or her. As a result, one of the keys to writing an effective resume is understanding the needs of employers. When your resume addresses the needs of an employer you will be more successful in marketing yourself.

When you understand what employers are looking for, and when you write a resume that shows you are the best person to meet these needs, you will find your greatest success. As your resume may often be your first contact with an employer, it is critical that the content of your resume addresses the question of what the employer is looking for. This might very well be the single most important thing to remember in writing a resume.

With more and more job applications being submitted online (often only asking for your resume), it is critical that your resume focuses on what the employer is looking for and how your education/training and skills make you the best person to fulfill the needs that the company has.

If you are the kind of person in the past who used the same resume for every job that you applied to, this was a mistake. Your resume should be individualized for every job that you apply for. We will look at how to do this later in this book. For now, simply keep in mind that every resume that you submit should be tailored specifically to the job (and company) that you are applying to. In my experience in working with unemployed people, those that had the most difficult time getting hired into a new job were those who kept using the same resume for every job they applied to without ever making any changes on it to reflect the needs of the company they were ap-

The most important question to be asking yourself when you write your resume is, "How can I best help this company?"

It is a serious mistake to keep using the same resume for every job that you apply to.

Your resume is a brief advertisement of who you are and how you can help the company you are applying to.

The goal of your resume is to get someone who does the hiring to give you an interview because your resume suggests you are the best person who can meet the needs of the company.

plying to. You will get help throughout this book in learning how to be more effective in writing a resume that is tailored specifically to the job and company you are applying to.

Too many people in seeking jobs are constantly asking, "How can this company best help me?" The question you should be asking yourself is, "How can I best help this company?" When the answer to this question becomes the foundation of the content of your resume, you will have a much stronger resume.

When I asked hundreds of companies what they were looking for when they hired new employees, the following six factors were those most frequently mentioned (and they are also in priority order with #1 being the factor that most employers stated was most important to them). In reading this list, it might be useful to realize that some jobs and some companies may rank these factors in a slightly different order and may even add additional factors, although the six factors listed here are important to keep in mind as you write your resume. In later chapters, I will show you how to incorporate these six insider secrets into your resume to make it more effective.

1. **TRAINING/QUALIFICATIONS**
2. **POSITIVE ATTITUDE**
3. **EXPERIENCE**
4. **PEOPLE SKILLS**
5. **WORK ETHIC**
6. **ADAPTABLE**

When you consider these six factors when you write your resume, you will have a much stronger resume. In the following chapters, you will be given an easy step-by-step format for doing this.

Applying for a job is a form of marketing. You are marketing yourself. Similar to any other form of marketing, you will be more successful if you understand the needs of your customers. In this case, your customer is your future employer. Take time to research their needs. Clues regarding their needs are found in job ads, company websites, newspaper/magazine articles regarding trends in your industry, and most of all by talking to people who are already in the career you are attempting to get hired into.

In this chapter I have shared six insider secrets that hundreds of companies have identified as being very important to them in hiring new employees. In the next few chapters we will begin to look at how you can integrate these secrets into your resume to make it more effective.

Before you move on to the next chapter, please complete Action Step #2 below.

Your resume should focus on how you can help the company, not how they can help you.

ACTION STEP #2

From your Job File, select any five job advertisements (if you haven't started your Job File, then now is the time to do this - see page 10 for instructions). Read the 5 job advertisements and look for any skills/traits/job requirements that are listed on more than one advertisement and write these words in the BOX 2 below. For example, if several of the advertisements said they were looking for someone who is a "team player" then you would write these words in the box below. If possible, identify and write at least three words or phrases that are repeated in at least some of the ads.

By looking at the company website or talking to people who work there, identify the kind of worker they value the most, and then ensure that your resume describes you as that kind of worker.

INSTRUCTIONS: After reading 5 job advertisements from your Job File, write any words or phrases that are repeated in some of the advertisements.

BOX 2

"Getting along with others is still the world's most needed skill. With it... there is no limit to what a person can do. We need people, we need the cooperation of others. There is very little we can do alone.

Earl Nightingale

WHAT ARE YOUR PERSONAL SKILLS?

In the previous chapter you looked at six insider secrets to help you better understand what employers are looking for when they hire new employers. By understanding what employers are looking for and by addressing these critical factors in your resume, you will develop a much stronger resume. In this chapter, you are going to look at your personal skills, and more specifically explore which personal skills are the most important to employers.

A dictionary might define "skill" as:

- expertise, practiced ability, something you do well

A thesaurus might define "skill" as:

- ability, adroitness, aptitude, competence, handiness

Your skills can generally be broken down into two main areas:

1. *Your Personal Skills*
2. *Your Job-Specific Skills*

Before going any further, let's make sure you understand the difference between your personal skills and your job-specific skills.

Your personal skills are sometimes referred to as your "soft skills". These include things like your ability to get along well with others, your attitude, your initiative, and your work ethic.

Your job-specific skills include things such as computer skills or any other skills that are specific to the job you are applying to. Most of your job-specific skills are the result of your education or training, although some of them might have also come from hobbies that you have.

"Natural ability is important, but you can go far without it if you have the focus, drive, desire and positive attitude."
Kirsten Sweetland

In the last chapter, you saw that the most important factor that employers want is that job applicants have the appropriate education or training for the job. In the next chapter we will focus on this in more detail. For now let's look at your personal skills. In the last chapter, the research I shared identified four personal skills that are important to employers. In review, these four skills are:

1. *Positive Attitude*
2. *People Skills*
3. *Work Ethic*
4. *Adaptable*

The content in this chapter can help you to better understand the personal skills that are important to employers. The "Action Activities" in this chapter will help you to list your best personal skills. Later in this book you will be shown how to add these to your resume.

Before you continue, just a reminder again that you should be adding a few new job advertisements into your "Job File" each day. This is important because you will be referring to these job advertisements later in this book.

Let's begin by looking at the number one personal trait that employers look for in a job applicant—Positive Attitude.

POSITIVE ATTITUDE

As you attempt to get a new job, you might have heard others say that "who you know is as important as what you know." Often, the people who find it easiest to get hired into a new job are the people who know someone who works in the company where they are applying. While some people think this is unfair, it is a reality in the workplace. By understanding the reason for this, you can better address it in your resume.

In research that I have done with hundreds of companies I found that the number one cause of stress in the workplace is conflict among co-workers (and next on the list were conflicts with a boss or even customers). Employers don't want to hire anyone who they think is going to be a cause of conflict in the workplace.

In most jobs, employers want people who are going to fit in with their co-workers. This is the number one reason why employers often hire friends or acquaintances of people who already work for the company. In these situations, it is unlikely that an employee is going to recommend a friend unless that friend gets along with others. This personal reference from an employee often carries more weight in hiring decisions than the normal references a person might list on their resume. In fact, it is not unusual when a job becomes available for an employer to ask her employees first if they know someone for the job even before it gets advertised (on the next page are some tips related to "fitting in").

As stated on the previous page, the number one personal skill that employers look for when they hire is positive attitude. The reality is that positive attitude also encompasses the other three personal skills that employers are looking for: people skills, work ethic, and adaptable.

Almost everyone who writes a resume says that they have "good people skills", they are a "good team player", they have a "positive attitude", and/or they are a "hard worker". It is often boring for an employer to keep hearing these same phrases repeated over and over. What can you say on your resume that will separate you from the other job applicants? Let's explore this further.

There are four major characteristics of positive people in the workplace. These are:

i) *They are 100% responsible for the work that they do.*

ii) *They like to solve problems.*

iii) *They work well with others.*

iv) *They are adaptable (or flexible).*

Let's look at each of these positive characteristics and then I will show you how to highlight this information on your resume.

> *"The greatest discovery of all time is that a person can change his future by merely changing his attitude."*
> Oprah Winfrey

"If we are basically positive in attitude, expecting and envisioning pleasure, satisfaction and happiness, we will attract people, and create situations and events which conform to our positive expectations."
Shakti Gawain

i) Being 100% responsible for the work that you do

People with a positive attitude accept 100% responsibility for their lives. They don't blame others when things go wrong. They accept personal responsibility for both successes and failures. When they try something and it doesn't work out the way they had hoped, instead of trying to find someone else to blame, they consider what they can learn from the experience and then begin again by adjusting their actions.

In addition, employees with a positive attitude are those who take the initiative to get their work done on time. These are the workers who are reliable, responsible, and punctual.

ii) Being a problem solver

There are always going to be problems in the workplace. Sometimes these problems are with co-workers, managers, or even customers. Other times the problems may focus on the quality of a product or service, or the process (or timelines) for providing a service or a product.

Most managers say that they spend most of their time "putting out fires" in the workplace. As a result of this time-consuming, stressful, part of their job they like to hire people who first of all don't regularly contribute to causing fires, but secondly who are good at solving problems so the manager doesn't always have to be the person who is putting out the fires.

In fact, a popular job interview question is: "Tell me about a problem you had with a co-worker or customer in a former job, and how you handled this." This question is an attempt by the employer to see if you have good problem solving skills.

iii) Working well with others

There are very few jobs today where an employee does not have to interact with others, whether it's co-worker or customers. In a job interview, you might even be asked: "Tell me what you would do as a new employee to fit in with the people who you work with." The information in this chapter can give you some thoughts on answering this question.

When you write your resume, you don't want to just say that you work well with others or that you are a team player, you want to provide specific evidence from a former job (or from school) that proves that you have this skill.

iv) *Being adaptable*
In a rapidly changing world, for any business to survive it must constantly adapt to new technologies and new ways of meeting customer needs. As a result, the most sought after employees are those who embrace change and like to learn. When an employee drags his heels and attempts to reject new ways of doing things, this costs both time and money for a business, and creates problems among co-workers. Being a flexible person can help you to be more successful in getting hired into a new job.

The information on the previous few pages gave you an overview of some of the components of having a positive attitude. Instead of simply saying you have a positive attitude on your resume, you can take the information from these pages and be more specific. Being specific about your skills can help you to have a more effective resume. Action Step #3 on page 27 will help you to do this.

The next five pages provides some tips or quotes related to "Positive Attitude", "Fitting In", "Tips for Dealing With Workplace Conflict", "Tips for Dealing with Change", and "Work Ethic". Read each of these pages before you attempt to complete Action Step #3 on page 27.

" An adaptable company is one that captures more than its fair share of new opportunities. It's always redefining its 'core business' in ways that open up new avenues of growth."
Gary Hamel

" The most successful people are those who accept, and adapt to constant change. This adaptability requires a degree of flexibility and humility most people can't manage."
Paul Lutus

Quotes Related To Positive Attitude

*"Optimism is the one quality more associated with success
and happiness than any other."*
Brian Tracy

*"Your own mind is a sacred enclosure into which nothing
harmful can enter except by your permission."*
Ralph Waldo Emerson

*"I have had dreams and I have had nightmares,
but I have conquered my nightmares because of my dreams."*
Dr. Jonas Salk

"If I keep a green bough in my heart, the singing bird will come."
Chinese Proverb

*"The optimist sees opportunity in every danger;
the pessimist sees danger in every opportunity."*
Winston Churchill

*"Happiness is an attitude. We either make ourselves miserable,
or happy and strong. The amount of work is the same."*
Francesca Reigler

*"There is a little difference in people, but that little difference
makes a big difference. That little difference is attitude.
The big difference is whether it is positive or negative."*
W. Clement Stone

*"All our dreams can come true -
if we have the courage to pursue them."*
Walt Disney

"You must do the thing you think you cannot do."
Eleanor Roosevelt

*"I am not discouraged, because every wrong attempt
discarded is another step forward."*
Thomas Edison

Tips On Fitting In

1. Find something good to say
about others if you have to say anything at all.

2. Do what you say you are going to do.
Honesty brings respect.

3. Show concern for the feelings of others.

4. Listen to others as they share their interests and ideas.

5. Be a positive person.
Leave your aches, pains and problems at home.

6. Be an optimistic person.
Look for the best in any situation instead of the worst.

7. Keep an open mind.
Learn to accept the differences in other people.

8. When you are presenting your point of view,
remain calm and deal with the facts.

9. Be quick to forgive.
If you have to confront a co-worker (or boss)
concerning a problem, do it in private
and at the convenience of the other person.

10. Take pride in your work
without feeling the need to boast about it.

Tips On Dealing With Workplace Conflict

1. Be proactive. Ignoring potential conflicts
can allow them to escalate.

2. Be slow to anger - especially over little things.
Listen before you speak. If necessary, go for a walk
or spend some time alone to relax before you deal with the conflict.

3. If you find that you are wrong, admit it. On the other hand, if you
are not wrong, be assertive in voicing your needs and rights.
Do not neglect your own needs in order to make other people happy.

4. Look at yourself first before you blame others.
Is there something you can do to resolve the concern
before it actually becomes a full blown problem?

5. Look for common ground as quickly as possible.

6. Attempt to understand the other person's point of view
rather than attempting to convince him/her of yours.
The most effective listening skill to use in understanding
another person is to paraphrase what he/she is telling you.

7. Where emotions are involved, let other people express
their feelings before you attempt to resolve the problem.

8. Attempt to handle the conflict in private instead of in front
of your co-workers. Avoid having anyone involved in the
conflict being embarrassed in front of others.

9. Avoid exaggerations, either in your mind or in what you say.
Attempt to keep your thoughts and words based on fact.

10. Look for solutions where both sides benefit.
It has been said that a winning solution is the art of dividing a cake
in such a way that everyone believes that they have the biggest piece.

Tips On Dealing With Change

1 Look for the opportunities and benefits
that the change can bring to you.

2. Don't waste energy on resisting change
if it's going to happen anyway.

3. Decide how to react to change rather than letting others
tell you how they think you should react.

4. Take responsibility for changing yourself,
not others.

5. Keep things in perspective.
We often allow things to become
much worse in our mind than they actually are.

6. Focus on what you can control, not what you cannot.

7. Learn how to deal with the stress of change
by employing techniques such as exercise or meditation.

8. Explore the different choices you have related to the change.

9. Get all the information related to the change
and attempt to understand it before you react.

10. Identify the emotions you are feeling,
and deal with them before you attempt
to work through the change.

Work Ethic Quotes

"I have missed more than 9,000 shots in my career.
I have lost almost 300 games. On 26 occasions I have been entrusted
to take the game winning shot ... and I missed.
I have failed over and over and over again in my life.
And that's precisely why I succeed."
Michael Jordan

"Nothing will ever be attempted if all possible objections
must first be overcome."
Samuel Johnson

"Doing the best at this moment
puts you in the best place for the next moment."
Oprah Winfrey

"Opportunity is missed by most because
it is dressed in overalls and looks like work."
Thomas Edison

"If people knew how hard I have to work to gain my mastery,
it wouldn't seem wonderful at all."
Michelangelo

"I'm a great believer in luck,
and I find the harder I work, the more I have of it."
Thomas Jefferson

"The only place where success comes before work is in the dictionary."
Vidal Sassoon

"I long to accomplish great and noble tasks, but it is my chief duty
to accomplish humble tasks as though they were great and noble."
Helen Keller

"The secret of joy in work is contained in one word - excellence."
Pearl S. Buck

"Pleasure in the job puts perfection in the work."
Aristotle

ACTION STEP #3

INSTRUCTIONS: In each chart below, there are 10 traits. In each chart, choose the **3** traits that best describe you and place them in the appropriate BOX underneath the chart. Your three traits in each BOX should be ranked with #1 being the word that best describes you, #2 being the word that next best describes you, and #3 being the word that next best describes you.

PEOPLE SKILLS

- optimistic
- rarely complains
- easy to get along with
- brings out the best in others
- good listener
- enjoys other people
- deals well with stress
- good problem solver
- respectful
- accepting of differences

WORK ETHIC

- achieves goals
- punctual
- organized
- responsible
- enthusiastic
- self-starter
- follows directions
- strong time management skills
- can work in a fast-paced work environment
- reliable

BEING ADAPTABLE

- flexible
- likes to learn
- embraces change
- quick learner
- good at multitasking
- open to suggestions
- learns from criticism
- not set in my ways
- enjoys a challenge
- understands that there are often different ways to solve a problem

PEOPLE SKILLS

From the above list, my top 3 PEOPLE SKILLS are:

1.

2.

3.

WORK ETHIC

From the above list, my top 3 WORK ETHIC traits are:

1.

2.

3.

ADAPTABLE

From the above list, my top 3 ADAPTABLE traits are:

1.

2.

3.

BOX 3

In Chapter 6, you will be shown how to enter this information on your resume.

*"Over the years, I've learned
that a confident person
doesn't concentrate or focus
on their weaknesses - they
maximize their strengths."*
Joyce Meyer

WHAT ARE YOUR
JOB-SPECIFIC SKILLS?

In my research with employers, 93.8% of them stated that the number one consideration in hiring new employees related to their qualifications and/or training credentials. What this really means is employers are looking for something concrete such as a diploma, certificate, license, or degree that proves that you have achieved the minimum standard required for the job they are advertising. In most cases, if you don't have this minimum standard you are wasting your time applying for the job. In fact, in my research with employers, one of the major concerns they have with people applying for jobs relates to those who apply for jobs even when they are not qualified. As you begin to market yourself to employers you want them to immediately recognize that you have the qualifications they are looking for.

It is critical to identify the basic educational or training qualifications required for a job when you look at a job advertisement. Do you have a certificate, diploma, or degree to prove that you have these qualifications? If not, are you prepared to return back to school to obtain these qualifications? In general, your qualifications can be shown by providing a certificate, diploma, license, or degree (or some other official piece of paper) that certifies that you have completed a required program in an accredited school or training facility.

Your education, training, and previous jobs have all helped you to learn job-specific skills. Most job advertisements state that job experience is required. If you have the job experience they are looking for, terrific. But if you don't, it may be that you have experiences in your education and training that can be used to show you have related job experience.

As you begin to think about your qualifications, it's important to realize that your qualifications are different than your skills. For ex-

You want the employer to immediately recognize that you have the qualifications they are looking for.

ample, typing 60 words a minute is a skill while graduating from a secretarial program states your qualifications. Knowing how to motivate children is a skill while completing a teacher education program proves your qualifications. Knowing how to wire a house is a skill while having completed an apprenticeship program as an electrician provides your qualifications. In this Chapter, you will identify the training or education that qualifies you for the job that you want, and then you will learn how to identify your job-specific skills. In later chapters, you will be shown how to add this information to your resume.

As you consider job advertisements, look closely for the educational level or training qualifications required for the jobs you are interested in. When you find a job that you might be interested in but you lack the qualifications, ask yourself whether you are prepared to gain these qualifications? If your answer is "no", then it might be in your best interest to begin to look for other jobs that you are qualified for.

ACTION STEP #4

INSTRUCTIONS: In BOX 4 below, list the training and/or educational qualifications you have and include the date(s) that you received this training or education. This would include any certificates, licences, diplomas, and/or degrees that you have.

My Educational and Training Qualifications

BOX 4

JOB-SPECIFIC SKILLS: The following are examples of specific job related skills employers might be looking for in a variety of jobs:

- proficient in using Microsoft Office Professional
- ability to install and maintain electrical equipment
- skills in coding
- knowledge of fabrication techniques
- experience in all phases of installation procedures
- good record keeping strategies
- strong database management skills
- driving experience
- can assemble mechanical components
- sound knowledge of related systems
- strong computer skills

On the following chart, list some of the job-specific skills that employers are asking for in most of the jobs in your Job File (and remember this list should focus on your job-specific skills and not your personal skills that you looked at in the last chapter).

Before you begin to write a resume, create a profile of what employers are looking for in the career you are seeking.

**Job-Specific Skills
That Employers Are Looking For**

On the previous page you identified the job-specific skills that employers were looking for. In BOX 5 below, list all the jobs (whether full-time or part-time), internships, and volunteer activities that you have participated in during the last 3 - 10 years.

> **ACTION STEP #5**
> **INSTRUCTIONS:** In BOX 5 below, list all the jobs, internships, and volunteer activities you have participated in during the past 3 - 10 years. Add the appropriate date(s) beside each listing.

My Employment History

BOX 5

"I'm not a product of my circumstances. I am a product of my decisions."
Stephen Covey

"A person who never made a mistake never tried anything new."
Albert Einstein

In this chapter you have identified your education and training qualifications (BOX 4 on page 30). You have also identified your employment history (BOX 5)). Next, you are going to identify your job-specific skills that best match the job-specific skills that employers are looking for (BOX 6 on the next page).

A theme throughout this book is that strong resumes (resumes that get results) are based on identifying what employers are looking for and then convincing the employer (through your resume) that you have the qualifications, the personal skills, and the job-specific skills that the employer s looking for. When you do this you will have a strong resume that can help you to be more successful in your job search.

ACTION STEP #6

INSTRUCTIONS: In BOX 6 below, identify the job-specific skills that you have that are the result of your past education/ training and former jobs/internsh ps or even volunteer work. In particular, identify any job-specific skills that you have that best match the skills employe-s are looking for in your job area (that you identified in the box at the bottom of page 31).

Job-Specific Skills

BOX 6

Now that you have identified your strengths (your education, your training, and your skills) in applying for a job, the next step is to prove what you are saying about yourself. The difference between a good resume and a great resume is one where you actually provide evidence that proves that you have the skills that you list (more on this in the next chapter).

*"Lasting accomplishment is
achieved through a long,
slow climb and self-discipline."*
Helen Hayes

IDENTIFYING YOUR ACCOMPLISHMENTS

CHAPTER

5

In the previous chapters you identified your qualifications, your personal skills, and your job-related skills. If you have been able to match your skills so far with what employers are looking for, your resume (that you will complete in Chapter 8) is already likely stronger than most others. There are two more things you can do to make your resume even more effective. The first is to identify accomplishments which prove what you have been saying about yourself (which you are going to do in this chapter). The second is to add keywords to your resume that you will do in the next chapter.

Your accomplishments are actual proof that you are able to employ your qualifications, your skills, your attitude and work ethic to do something meaningful. You might have said (back in Chapter 3 when we looked at personal skills) that you are a good team player. This is a claim that many people make on their resumes, especially if the job advertisement said that the employer was looking for someone who is a "team player." In this instance, you can make yourself (through your resume) stand out from other job applicants by providing some kind of proof that you are a team player. For example, you might say something along the lines of the following:

- contributed to our sales team to exceed our goals
- assisted our advertising team in creating a new ad campaign
- helped our office team prioritize what we had to do
- worked as part of a team to achieve our monthly goals
- was part of a successful team in implementing a new project

In each of the above statements, the word "team" is used, but instead of just saying you are a good team player you mention a specific example of when you were actually part of a successful team. The comments I provided are fairly general. You could make such statements even more powerful if you named the goals, the projects, or used some actual statistics or data to support what you are saying. If you are a student, you could use an example from a group

"Champions keep playing until they get it right."
Billie Jean King

RESUME RESULTS
35

project at school, your involvement in some extracurricular activity, volunteering in the community, or even from a part-time job experience.

In your resume, employers are often looking for specific things you have accomplished in previous jobs (for students, part-time jobs or school/community related accomplishments can be used). These accomplishments support the other things you have said about yourself on your resume.

Examples of your accomplishments might be projects or tasks you completed (whether as an individual or part of a team) that you felt really good about. Accomplishments may also include new ideas or proposals that you made that resulted in concrete products or improvements of some form. Accomplishments may also include successfully solving problems, whether product or people related. In addition, accomplishments could include anything you did that improved the company profile in a positive way or increased company profits, or even some small thing you did to help a co-worker be more successful.

Your accomplishments could also focus on successfully helping customers which could support your claims about having good "people skills." Almost everyone states that they have good "people skills" on their resume. The most effective resumes state an accomplishment that proves you have strong people skills. The following provide some examples of things you might say about your involvement with customers.

- helped a frustrated customer find the product she was looking for
- helped resolve a situation involving an angry customer
- helped a confused customer understand how to use one of our products
- helped sell a major product to one of our customers
- helped a customer better understand our product warranty

In some situations, your accomplishments may have resulted in you receiving an award or some other form of recognition (prize, bonus, media coverage, letter, verbal congratulations, etc.). Such accomplishments are the best ones to use when you are trying to make a positive impact on a future employer.

The following four Activity Steps will provide some practice for you in identifying some of your accomplishments.

ACTION STEP #7

INSTRUCTIONS: In the following box (BOX 7), list any awards or other forms of recognition you have received during your education or in a previous job.

Recognition and Awards that I Have Received

BOX 7

ACTION STEP #8

INSTRUCTIONS: In the following box (BOX 8), list a few examples you can think of that prove that you have good "people skills".

Proof that I have Good People Skills

BOX 8

"Small daily improvements over time lead to stunning results."
Robin Sharma

"Achievement seems to be connected with action. Successful men and women keep moving. They make mistakes, but they don't quit."
Conrad Hilton

ACTION STEP #9

INSTRUCTIONS: In the following box (BOX 9), list a few examples you can think of that prove that you are a good "team player".

Proof that I'm a Good Team Player

BOX 9

Our accomplishments are the proof that we are not just idle dreamers.

ACTION STEP #10

INSTRUCTIONS: In the following box (BOX 10), list a few examples you can think of that prove that you have a strong "work ethic". You might refer back to page 27 for help.

BOX 10

Your work on the previous two pages will be helpful to you when you complete your resume in Chapter 8. Next, you are going to look at how keywords can strengthen your resume

Accomplishment Quotes

*"In the confrontation between the stream and the rock,
the stream always wins, not by strength but through perseverance."*
H. J. Brown

*"It is by what we ourselves have done,
and not by what others have done for us,
that we shall be remembered in after ages."*
Francis Wayland

"It is not so important who starts the game but who finishes it."
John Wooden

*"To be yourself in a world that is constantly trying to make you
something else is the greatest accomplishment."*
Ralph Waldo Emerson

"Discipline is the bridge between goals and accomplishment."
Jim Rohn

*"Nothing stops the man who desires to achieve.
Every obstacle is simply a course to develop his achievement muscle."*
Eric Butterworth

*"Not everyone desires to be a bank president or a nuclear scientist,
but everyone wants to do something with one's life
that will give him a sense of pride and accomplishment."*
Ronald Regan

*"Every great work, every big accomplishment
has been brought into manifestation through holding to
the vision, and often just before the big achievement,
comes apparent failure and discouragement."*
Florence Shinn

"Nothing will ever work unless you do."
Maya Angelou

"Depending on how a specific ATS (applicant tracking system) works, the location and frequency of keywords within your resume can be extremely important."

Deanna Hartley
(Career Builder)

THE IMPORTANCE
OF KEYWORDS

In the past, your resume was one of the first steps in making a first impression on a potential future employer. Many companies now use software to screen resumes, so instead of attempting to make your first impression on a human, you might need to make it on a robot. When you submit your resume, it may be scanned by the use of an Applicant Tracking Systems (ATS) which is software designed to look for keywords that an employer desires in a resume. If your resume doesn't have the keywords that an employer is looking for, your resume may never reach a human. It's been estimated that ATS is used by more than 95% of Fortune 500 companies.

To help you beat the algorithms in an ATS, there are some basic strategies to consider in writing your resume. ATS works by looking for keywords in a resume that are important to the company that has posted the job. If the ATS software finds that your resume has 5 keywords while some other resume has 10 keywords, then this resume will likely get further attention at the company. One of the most important ways to identify keywords is through a careful reading of the job advertisement.

Completing the following activity can help you to begin to understand how to identify keywords.

If your resume doesn't have the keywords that an employer is looking for, your resume may never reach a human.

ACTION STEP #11
INSTRUCTIONS: Read the following job advertisement, and underline what you think are the keywords.

Sales Associate: *The main requirements are providing excellent customer services, applying store operations policies, working closely with store management and store selling team, experience with high-end clients, proven sales track record, achievement of sales goals, three years experience, multilingual (Spanish and Chinese preferred, strong decision making skills, strong computer skills, and strong collaboration skills*   **BOX 11**

The chart below lists the keywords you might have underlined on the previous page. How well did you do?

Job Advertisement Keywords (from page 41)

- excellent customer services
- store operations policies
- works closely with store management
- works closely with store selling team
- experience with high-end clients
- proven sales track record

- achievement of sales goals
- three years experience
- multilingual (Chinese + Spanish)
- strong decision making skills
- strong computer skills
- strong collaboration skills

Using the previous job advertisement as an example, you want to employ as many of these keywords in your bullet points on your resume so using the above chart as a guide, you might state some of the following:

- proven sales track record with high-end clients
- works well with management and store selling teams
- won an award for customer services
- top salesperson of the year in achieving my goals

You will notice that in some of the above points, keywords phrases have been combined. In addition, where possible any accomplishments that relate to the keywords have been added. Remember from the last chapter that accomplishments can be very important to include in your resume as they prove that you actually have the skills you are talking about.

Some advertisements may have so many keywords that you are going to have to prioritize what you think are the most important. At other times, if the advertisement has few keywords, it might be useful to create synonyms for the words that you do have. Scatter your keywords throughout your resume, and if you are also submitting a cover letter, insert keywords in this as well.

In thinking about which keywords to use on your resume, you

might also find it helpful to identify keywords from other job advertisements in the same field as the job you are applying to. Where you see keywords being repeated in several advertisements, these are often good keywords to emphasize on your resume.

It is often useful to repeat the most important keywords a few times on your resume, but don't overdo it; ATS algorithms can identify and discard resumes that keep repeating one or two keywords.

An important point to remember related to your use of keywords (any other information on your resume) is don't lie. If you are successful in obtaining a job interview, your resume will often be used by the interviewer in asking questions. If you have said something on your resume that turns out to be a lie, this will likely prevent you from getting the job. You can't be expected to be able to fulfill 100% of the keywords in the job advertisement. Select the keywords that best apply to you and insert them into your resume along with a related accomplishment, if possible, to actually prove that you have the skill you have listed.

In submitting an online application, it is important to keep your resume formatting simple. Obscure fonts and pictures may present a problem for the company's ATS which could result in you resume being rejected. When submitting a resume online, read the expectations carefully for formatting. Generally you will be asked to submit your resume as a PDF or Word file. Don't submit your file in a format that is different than what you are being asked for. There will be more information provided on formatting an online resume in the next chapter.

ATS software is designed to determine which resumes will actually move on to be seen by a human. If you know someone who works in the company you are applying to, you might be able to bypass the ATS system by contacting this person and telling them that you are submitting a resume for a job at this company. This person can then alert someone in "hiring" who will then watch for your resume. This way, your resume might be seen by a human regardless of how the ATS software responds to it.

"No longer are human resource managers scouring resumes looking for intriguing phrases on luxurious linen paper. Now, resumes are downloaded into a database and digitally searched for specific keywords. If your resume doesn't contain the keywords the employer is looking for, consider yourself overlooked."
Humboldt State University, Academic & Career Advising Centre

"Recruiters have a job to do and need to do it quickly, which is why it is critical that they be able to assess your experience, education, and skills in just a few seconds. Having a great resume format is critical to organizing your information in a way that will help you get noticed."

LiveCareer

FORMATTING YOUR RESUME

How to best format your resume is an evolving process. Not too long ago, it was expected that resumes should be submitted on paper with specific formatting rules. Now that more and more resumes are being submitted online, the rules are changing. In this chapter, information will be provided on formatting paper resumes as well as digital resumes. While the content of both resumes remains the same, there are some differences in how these resumes should be formatted. There are books and websites (some of these websites are identified on the next page) that provide dozens and dozens of sample resumes. While it might be useful to consider the styles of various resumes when they are going to be on paper, for the purpose of a digital resume the formatting should be straightforward and kept as simple as possible. Information will also be presented in this chapter on video resumes which may become a trend in the future for some industries.

As has already been mentioned, the key for having a successful resume relates to having content that best meets the needs of an employer, and this is often done by using keywords and accomplishments (as discussed in the last two chapters) as well as focusing on your best personal and job-specific skills (as identified in Chapters 3 + 4).

A rule of thumb for successful paper resumes would be writing a resume that looks professional. A rule of thumb for successful digital resumes would be submitting a resume where the formatting remains constant. This chapter can help you to format either resume in a manner that meets these basic expectations.

PAPER RESUMES: First of all, let's look at paper resumes. Even if you are expected to submit a digital resume, it's often a good idea to create a paper resume first because you can cut and paste information from the paper resume into a digital resume.

Your resume represents you. How you present it conveys part of who you are to a potential employer.

www.indeed.com

www.careerbuilder.com

www.myperfectresume.com

www.resumecoach.com

https://resume.io/templates

https://zety.com

https://resumegenius.com

www.monster.com

https://livecareer.com

Page 47 provides some tips on writing a paper resume. One of the keys with a paper resume is creating a resume that looks professional, although in the end, it is the content that is most important. Having said this, though, if your paper resume looks cluttered or has coffee stains (or even photocopying marks) on it, it might be discarded before an employer even reads it. It is expected that paper resumes are on white paper and that there is a clean, easy-to-read look to them. The sample paper resume on pages 48 + 49 can help you examine a professional looking paper resume, while the website links on the left hand side of this page can give you access to free resume templates that you might want to use.

In my work with thousands of job-seekers, those who struggled to get results from their resumes were often those who wrote one resume and then simply photocopied hundreds of copies of this resume to send out. Your resume must be specifically tailored for every new job that you apply for, using keywords from each job advertisement and often changing the wording for the position you are applying for. These changes may appear to be minor but they can make a huge difference in how the resume is perceived by the person receiving it. A mass produced resume is rarely well received. Small changes in your resume to show that it has been written specifically for the company you are applying to is an important part of having an effective resume.

As with any other aspect of your job search, attempt to get feedback from others regarding your resume. It would be particularly helpful to have people who you may know who are actually involved in hiring for their company give you feedback related to your resume. Counselors/advisors at career centers can also assist you in assessing your resume. Keep in mind that the main purpose of your resume is to help you get a job interview. If you are sending out dozens of resumes, but you are not getting any interviews, it may be that you need to revise your resume. In such a situation, a career counselor or advisor at a local community college or career center could be very helpful to you.

Next, we will look at some tips related to preparing a digital resume to be submitted online. These tips begin on page 50.

Tips for Writing a Paper Resume

1. Your resume creates a first impression. Use good quality 8 1/2 X 11" white bond paper. Use a laser-quality printer to provide clean, clear copies.

2. Use basic fonts such as Times New Roman, Arial, or Calibri. Use a font size of about 12. Don't use more than two fonts in your resume.

3. Keep your resume to no more than two pages. A crowded resume is difficult to read. Keep your resume simple and inviting. White space can help keep the resume attractive and easy to read.

4. Don't lie on your resume and don't exaggerate. Whatever you write on your resume is often referred to in job interviews. Only write content that you can prove if you are asked about it.

5. Avoid using the word "I". Using point form instead of sentences can help you with this.

6. Your resume should emphasize your skills and accomplishments that relate to the job you are applying for. Use keywords from the job advertisement throughout your resume.

7. Don't include your height, weight, age, date of birth, place of birth, marital status, health, ethnicity/race, religion, social security number, or other such personal information.

8. Don't be too wordy. Often, less is more.

9. Target your resume to the position you are applying for. Don't write one that you use over and over again for many different jobs. Match your resume to the job advertisement.

10. Ensure that you have no spelling or grammatical errors.

MICHELLE WYSNEWKINSKI

3764 Valleyview Ave   Rochester   NY   14890
Telephone: (555) 787-0934   Email: mwysnewkinski@turbospeed.com

JOB OBJECTIVE: Public Relations Manager

PERSONAL SKILLS:
- received an Industry Media Award for constantly exceeding expectations
- often selected by management to troubleshoot conflict concerns with customers
- self-starter, works well in a fast-paced environment
- as team chairperson helped to increase customer base by 36.3%
- assistant manager of 8 that saw a reduction of 64% in absenteeism over 3 years
- as a member of the company administrative team we exceeded sales goals over a two year period by 18.6%
- presented workshops at 7 conferences over past two years on "Establishing Customer Loyalty"

JOB-SPECIFIC SKILLS

- excellent proficiency with all aspects of Microsoft Office Professional, Adobe Photoshop, Final Cut Pro, and Adobe Illustrator
- strong analytical and listening skills to assist in identifying the needs of customers and to offer positive solutions to customer concerns and perceptions
- excellent presentation skills including the mastery of workshop presentations, video production techniques, and web conferencing
- familiarity with designing needs based surveys, interpreting the data of such surveys, and implementing programs to address the identified needs
- excellent skills in motivating other team members to reach department goals
- excellent communication skills appropriate to a wide range of media possibilities including but not limited to television, radio, Internet, and print

WORK EXPERIENCE:

Kelly Marketing Group - Assistant Public Relations Manager   2015 to present

West Coast Media Group - Public Relations   2013 - 2015

MICHELLE WYSNEWKINSKI

Telephone: (555) 787-0934   Email: mwysnewkinski@turbospeed.com

OTHER RELATED WORK EXPERIENCE:

National Post - Public Relations Internship   2012 - 2013

Brown College - Assistant Advertising Manager (part-time), College newspaper   2010 - 2012

Brown College - Advertising Sales Rep., College newspaper (part-time position)   2008 - 2010

EDUCATION/TRAINING:

Brown College - B.A., major in Media Communications (Honors Standing)   2008 - 2012
- top class marks in 3 different senior level communication courses
- received a Brown College Media Communications Scholarship
- received the J. Proctor Award for outstanding work in Media
  Communications studies

Central High School - Honors Graduation Diploma   2004 - 2008

ASSOCIATION MEMBERSHIPS

Human Resources Professional Association   2013 to present

Association of Professional Public Relations Managers   2016 to present
- current Vice-President of local chapter

REFERENCES

- school and business references available upon request

In looking at the sample resume on the past two pages, there are a few things to recognize. First, there is a neat, orderly appearance with white space (white space prevents your resume from looking cluttered, thus making it easier to read, and this also provides space for an employer to make notes). Also note that the person's name and contact information is at the top of both pages (and the font for this information is consistent). Throughout the resume, the font type (and size) used for the headings is consistent as is the font type and size for the information presented. Finally, this person has provided data and other forms of accomplishment to prove what she is saying about herself. Most of her information is specific, rather than making vague comments about her people skills or work ethic.

DIGITAL RESUME: The content that was included in the paper resume on pages 48 + 49 would remain the same for a digital resume. The only difference would be in how the resume is formatted. A digital resume may be submitted online as part of your job application or it could be posted on any social media sites you belong to such as Linkedin or career sites such as Monster.

The most important aspect of formatting a digital resume is understanding the format you are being asked for. In some cases, you will be expected to attach your resume as a PDF or Word file so if this is the stated expectation, don't submit your file as a Google document or from a MAC specific program. If your resume is not submitted in the required file form, it will not even be looked at.

Sometimes, in applying for online jobs, you will be required to enter your information into the headings that an employer provides for you. In situations like this, it is still recommended that you initially prepare a complete resume so that you can proof it. Once you have done this, you can then cut and paste your resume into the appropriate boxes that are provided online by the company.

The following page provides some other tips on creating an effective digital resume, although the key is to first write this resume using the content tips that have been provided throughout this book. Chapter 8 will help you to do this.

Tips for Submitting Online Resumes

1. Follow the instructions precisely.

2. Don't use obscure fonts, logos, headers and footers.

3. Submit your resume in the expected format (generally PDF or Word).

4. Attempt to make a personal contact with someone at the company. If you have a personal connection, call them to let them know that you are submitting your resume. This person can tell "hiring" to watch for your resume. This approach can help you to get past the ATS.

5. In addition to identifying keywords from the job advertisement, look at related job advertisements that might also give you some hints on keywords that are important in the job field you are looking at.

6. If you are cutting and pasting your resume into an online submission box, use plain text with no fancy fonts or formatting.

7. If the advertisement doesn't say anything about a cover letter, it is usually a good idea to submit one if possible as this is an opportunity to expand on a few key points from your resume (and increase your use of keywords).

8. Keep your Linkedin profile up-to-date, and ensure that any profiles on any social media (such as Facebook) supports all the things you have said about yourself on your resume. If your social media sites don't support your resume, either update them or change your filters as to who can see your profile.

9. Use a professional email address. You might have an unusual email address that you use with your friends, but don't use this on your resume.

10. Send your resume from your home computer, rather than from a workplace computer. Using a workplace computer to apply for a job at another company could jeopardize your current job. Send a copy of your resume to yourself or a friend by email to ensure that the formatting doesn't change when the resume is sent electronically.

VIDEO RESUME: Many of the tips that have been said so far in this chapter related to the content of your resume also holds true for video resumes. As recommended for digital resumes, it is also suggested that in making a video resume that you first of all make a paper resume. Your paper resume can provide an outline of some of the things you would like to include in your video resume. Similar to the discussion in the last few chapters of this book, your video resume should highlight your accomplishments which should support the keywords that were presented in the job advertisement.

If you are expected to submit a digital (or paper) resume in addition to your video resume, your video resume does not have to be an exact repetition of your other resume. Your video resume can actually show you doing some of the things you have talked about in your other resume. It can also show examples of your work and accomplishments (provided they relate to the job you are applying to).

If you are not expected to submit a video resume, you can still have links to your website or to YouTube in your paper or digital resume that illustrate examples of your work.

Keep in mind that if you are making a video resume, it must look professional. Your resume is a reflection of who you are and the kind of employee you will be. An unprofessional, poorly made video can create problems for you.

An online video can help an employer to better understand your personality which is often an important part of getting a job. As explained back in Chapter 3, employers generally want to hire people who will get along with others in the workplace. If your video could include you working with others (whether customers or co-workers), this could be helpful to you. The important bottom line here is that you present yourself as an enthusiastic (but not over-the-top) positive person.

In making a video, it's critical that you have the potential to edit the scenes that you film. It is strongly recommended that you find someone who has the appropriate skills in filming and editing your video. The following page provides some further tips.

Tips on Creating a Video Resume

1. Only submit a video resume if this is what you are being asked to do, although you could have links in your paper or online resume that could show an employer samples of your work, or samples of you performing related work. For example, if you were applying for a job as an entertainer, it would definitely be useful to have online links in your resume that actually show you performing.

2. If at all possible, have your video shot and edited by someone who has training and appropriate skills to create a professional looking video.

3. Sound is very important in a video resume. Ensure that there is no troublesome background noise and that the position of your microphone captures your voice clearly. Keep in mind that cameras that have built in microphones sometimes capture the internal sound of the camera which can be annoying in attempting to listen to what you are saying.

4. Dress in your video interview as though you were in the actual workplace.

5. Pay attention to the background in your video. You don't want the employer to see possible inappropriate posters or pictures on the wall behind you that don't convey a positive image about you.

6. It is a good idea to prepare a script that incorporates the best of your resume (and also focuses on the keywords from the job advertisement).

7. Address the needs of the employer, rather than your needs. And keep in mind that this is a video that is intended to help you get a job, not a video that highlights your personal life.

8. Attempt to show, rather than brag. Avoid making jokes; you have no idea of what kind of humor your employer might enjoy.

9. Unless otherwise state, your video should be less than 3 minutes (and 1 - 2 minutes is better).

10. Get feedback from others before you submit your video.

"Learning how to write a killer resume can ratchet up your job search, cement your status as a top notch candidate, and increase your chances of landing a new gig. In other words, it's a major game changer."

Time, Careers

WRITING YOUR RESUME

Congratulations! You are now ready to write your resume. If you employ the tips from previous chapters, you can end up with an effective resume that will hopefully bring you good results. The sample resume provided in this chapter could easily be set up in Microsoft Word, and as a result could be submitted as either a paper resume or as a digital resume.

If you have completed all the "Action Steps" throughout this book it should be easy for you to take this information and insert it under the appropriate headings in the sample resume that is provided on pages 57 + 58. If you have not completed all the Action Steps, you may have to back and complete them. The information from these activities is very important in creating a strong resume.

Once you have completed the resume on pages 57 + 58, you could transfer this content into any resume template that you wish to use (such as the ones from the free template links on page 46). You could also transfer this information into a Word file to use as a digital resume (submitting it as either a Word file or PDF depending on what the online resume instructions tell you to do).

To complete the resume on pages 57 + 58, you will first of all need a job advertisement. This can come from your Job File that you have been completing throughout this book, or you can select a new advertisement for a current job that you would like to apply to.

Page 56 provides a step-by-step process for completing your resume. Follow it carefully and you will end up with a resume that should be beneficial to you in your job search.

If you are a student or someone with little job experience, you might find that you will end up with a one-page resume instead of two. You can still complete pages 57 + 58 and then condense this information into one page (more on this on page 59).

"Emphasize your strengths on your resume. It may sound obvious, but you'd be surprised how many people simply list everything they've ever done. Convey your passion and link your strengths to measurable results. Employers and interviewers love concrete data."
Marcus Buckingham

A Step-by-Step Guide for Writing Your Resume

1. Write your name, address, telephone number, and email address at the top of both page 57 + 58. When you enter this information into Word, you could "bold" your name, increase the font size of your name to 14, and use a different font than you use for the body of your resume. As you complete your resume, you could refer back to pages 48 + 49 to see how a completed resume looks. If you are submitting a paper resume or a PDF file online, you could add the lines in between your name and address. For the remainder of your resume, keep your font size to 12 and bold your headings.

2. State the name of the job you are applying for under the heading "Job Objective" on page 57.

3. From BOX 3 on page 27, list your personal skills on page 57 under the heading of "Personal Skills". The skills that you list should be the ones that best match the personal skills mentioned in the job advertisement. Where possible, use keywords from the job advertisement and also where possible add any accomplishments or forms of recognition that support any of your personal skills. You can refer back to BOXES 7, 8, 9, and 10 on pages 37 + 38 to help you add supporting evidence to the personal skills that you list here.

4. From BOX 6 on page 33, add your job-specific skills under the heading "Job-Specific Skills" on page 57. In addition, add any other job-specific skills you have that were included in the job advertisement.

5. From BOX 5 on page 32, list your employment history under "Work Experience" on page 57. If you have no full-time work experience, list part-time jobs, internships, or related volunteer activities. If you have several examples of full-time work experience, then your part-time work, internships, and related volunteer activities could be listed under the heading "Other Related Work Experience" on page 58.

6. From BOX 4 on page 30, write your education and training qualification on page 58 under the heading of "Education/Training". Make sure that you include the actual names of any certificates, licenses, diplomas, or degrees that you have received along with the dates of completing them.

7. Using BOX 7 on page 37 as a guide, add any awards or other forms of recognition under the heading "Other" on page 58. Add the dates beside each form of recognition. If you have nothing to add here, you could delete this heading, or change it to "Memberships" or "Interests", but generally interests are only used on a resume if there is some direct relationship between your interests and your personal or job-specific skills. Any accomplishments or forms of recognition could also be added to support your "Personal and Job-Specific Skills" on page 57.

8. Reread the job advertisement several times, underlining the keywords. Check your resume to ensure that you have used the main keywords throughout your resume.

9. Proof your resume for accuracy, grammar and spelling.

10. Have a friend or an employment counsellor proof your resume.

Telephone: Email:

JOB OBJECTIVE:

PERSONAL SKILLS:

JOB-SPECIFIC SKILLS

WORK EXPERIENCE:

Telephone: Email:

OTHER RELATED WORK EXPERIENCE:

EDUCATION/TRAINING:

OTHER

REFERENCES

   - references available upon request

You have now completed your resume. The next step is to take your rough draft on pages 57 + 58 and transfer this information to a Word document or into a resume template (see page 46)

As you look at resume templates, it's possible that some headings may be different than the ones you used on pages 57 + 58, but the main headings should be the same or similar.

If you are a student or someone who has very little full-time job experience then it is okay to have a one-page resume. In such a situation, you would eliminate any of the headings where you have no information, and you would have a reduced number of points under your other headings. Any internships or volunteer experiences could go under the heading of "Work Experience". If you have a one-page resume, you should still have the following headings:

- Job Position
- Personal Skills
- Job-Specific Skills
- Work Experience
- Training/Education
- References

Although this book has focused on helping you to write an effective resume, there are other important components of being successful in your job search. The final chapter in this book will provide some tips on other aspects of your job search.

"So, should a resume be one page, or two? I have good news. There's an answer. It just depends on how many years' experience you've got."
Tom Gerencer, Zety

"Good luck is when opportunity meets preparation, while bad luck is when lack of preparation meets reality."

Eliyahu Goldratt

OTHER JOB SEARCH TIPS

Although the focus of this book has been on creating an effective resume, resumes are not the only part of your job search. The basic purpose of a resume is to help you get a job interview. Another purpose of your resume is to provide an overview of who you are that could become the basis on what you talk about in a job interview. This final chapter will focus on some other aspects of a successful job search beyond your resume.

"There's more to a job search than simply applying for online postings, though the majority of job seekers confine their job search to exactly that."
Career Centre,
York University

Searching for a job is a form of marketing; you are marketing yourself. As explained earlier in this book, employers love to hire people who have a personal connection with someone in their company. As you apply for jobs, anyone you come into contact with (relatives, neighbors, friends, people at the gym, etc.) could be a potential connection to an employer. Page 62 provides some tips on networking effectively with others while page 63 provides some tips on marketing yourself.

Job interviews are often recognized as the most stressful part of applying for a job. Page 64 provides some tips on preparing for a job interview. Page 65 provides some tips on handling different kinds of job interviews. Pages 66 + 67 provide 50 typical job interview questions. Pages 68 + 69 provide sample answers for ten of the most frequently asked questions in a job interview. Page 70 provides some tips on dealing with the stress of job interviews.

Good luck in your job search! I wish you the best (and there are some quotes on good luck found on page 71).

NETWORKING TIPS

As you begin to look for your perfect job, you will constantly be talking to others (whether it's family, relatives, neighbors, friends, potential employers, etc.). This is known as "networking". As you network with others (even if you don't think the other person has any connection with someone who may hire you), always present yourself as someone who is optimistic and as someone who is qualified for the job that you are seeking.

Whenever you create a positive impression with another person, you will be quickly remembered if this person knows someone who might be able to help you in your job search. If you create a negative impression by complaining about how hard it is to find a job or just by being generally pessimistic, this person might listen to your concerns, but then make a mental note not to ever recommend you to someone who might be able to help you.

You never know who might provide a personal link to a potential employer, so strive to impress everyone who you talk to.

In addition, whenever someone takes the time to help you in your job search it would be beneficial for you to send them a thank-you card. People like to receive cards that thank them for making an extra effort to help someone else. Often, such a card may be posted in the person's office and becomes a reminder of your desire to find the job of your dreams.

By sending a thank-you card, you are helping to enhance your image as a positive person who is willing to give thanks and acknowledge the efforts of others. You can purchase blank thank-you cards at most drug stores or stationary stores. Don't choose a card that is too flashy or uses humor that could be interpreted the wrong way. Simply find a card that says thank you. If possible, use a quality printer to print your name, address, telephone number and email address inside the card. And don't forget as you thank the person to remind them once again of the actual job you are seeking.

Local community colleges and/or employment centers often offer free workshops related to writing resumes, job interviews, etc. You might find it very helpful to participate in these workshops, and as a bonus the counselors at these centers often receive information on current job postings.

TIPS FOR MARKETING YOURSELF

1. First impressions are important.
Always create a positive image of yourself.

2. Dress for success.

3. Take care of yourself through good eating,
sleeping and exercise habits.

4. Set a daily schedule that outlines
your goals each day in looking for a job.

5. Work hard at understanding exactly
what a company is looking for and then match
your job search efforts to meet these needs.

6. Learn as much as you can about the company you are applying to.
Ask yourself how you can contribute to this company's success.

7. Identify someone who either works for, or knows someone
who works for the company you are interested in.
Talk to this person about the company's needs.

8. Form a buddy group with other people who are looking for a job.
Help each other with job searching, resumes, practice interviews, etc.

9. Be persistent, but also be willing to change your approach
if you are not getting the results you would like.

10. Get help from a counselor at a career center.
Be positive with everyone you talk to about getting a job.

TIPS ON PREPARING FOR A JOB INTERVIEW

1. Ensure you know the time, date and location
for your interview. If possible, learn the names and positions
of those who will be interviewing you. By driving to the
company a few days before your interview you can ensure
you know how long it takes to get there as well as
viewing what employees are wearing.

2. A key to impressing anyone is being confident.
It is easier to be confident when you have prepared
answers to potential questions and practiced answering them.
Research the company, and also be prepared to talk about
what a person does in the position you are applying for.

3. Read and reread your resume and cover letter preparing
specific examples from previous job experiences to illustrate
the things you have said about yourself.

4. Read the job advertisement several times.
Highlight the important aspects of what the company
is looking for and think about how you can include
this information in your answers to questions.

5. Prepare a list of questions you would like to ask the company.

6. Dress for success. When you feel good about what you are wearing,
you will be more confident. Avoid perfumes, excessive jewelry,
and avoid smoking immediately before an interview.

7. Have paper, a quality pen, your resume, your questions,
any reference letters, or other supporting documents
ready the night before.

TIPS FOR DIFFERENT INTERVIEW TYPES

TELEPHONE INTERVIEW: These are sometimes used to screen applicants to decide who will actually get an interview. Keep your answers brief, but always attempt to support what you are saying by giving specific examples. Keep your resume handy as a guide for such an interview.

ONE-TO-ONE INTERVIEW: These are traditionally the most common form of interview. Maintain comfortable eye contact and address the interviewer by name.

GROUP INTERVIEW: Write down the names of the people interviewing you. Focus on the person who has asked you the current question. Make a positive impression on the group one person at a time.

SERIAL INTERVIEW: Sometimes you may be interviewed by several people but not necessarily at the same time. Keep notes on your answers after each interview so you are consistent in your responses.

VIDEO CONFERENCING INTERVIEW: In general, prepare for the interview as though you were in a room with the actual person. Speak clearly. Avoid bright colors. Maintain eye contact with the camera. If this is being conducted over the Internet, ensure you are using a dependable computer and connection. In addition, if you will be at home for this interview, consider what is in the room or on the wall behind you that will also show up in the interview.

AUDITION INTERVIEW: In this interview you may be asked to demonstrate some of your actual skills. Make sure you understand what you are being asked to do before you begin any task. Remain calm and focused on the task.

MEANDERING INTERVIEW: Occasionally, you might be interviewed by someone who has trouble maintaining a focus in the interview. In such situations, look for opportunities to provide answers to the major questions you were expecting even if they are not asked.

MEAL TIME INTERVIEW: In some situations, you may be required to join an interviewer during lunch or dinner. In such a situation, there may be an emphasis on looking at your social skills. Takes cues from your interviewer as to when to sit down, etc. Avoid stories or jokes that present you or anyone else in a bad manner.

SAMPLE JOB INTERVIEW QUESTIONS

As you experience job interviews (or talk to others who have been through job interviews), keep a list of your own job interview questions. In addition, explore the Internet for other samples of interview questions. The following provide some of the most often used generic questions that might be "skill" or "knowledge" based for specific careers.

1. Tell me about yourself.
2. What do you know about our company?
3. What do you know about the expectations of the job you are applying for?
4. Why should we hire you?
5. Where do you see yourself as being in 5 years?
6. What do other people generally say about you?
7. What would former employers say about you?
8. What would former co-workers say about you?
9. Tell me about a difficult situation you handled well in a former job.
10. Tell me about a significant achievement you made in a former job.
11. Give me an example of a task you had to complete under pressure.
12. Tell me how you handle stress.
13. What kinds of decisions do you find the most difficult to make?
14. Why did you leave your last job?
15. What are your strengths?
16. What are your weaknesses?
17. Why do you want to work here?
18. How do you stay professionally current?
19. How would you best describe your ideal job?
20. What do you think it takes to be successful in this job?
21. Describe a time you worked successfully as part of a team.
22. What motivates you?
23. Give me an example when you used good judgment to solve a problem.
24. Give me an example when you had to work
with someone who didn't like you.
25. What would you do if a co-worker
was not doing his/her share of the work?

SAMPLE JOB INTERVIEW QUESTIONS

26. What steps would you follow to solve a problem?
27. Describe a time when you were not very satisfied
with your work performance.
28. Have you done this type of work before?
29. What is the salary that you expect?
30. How would you handle a situation with an angry customer or co-worker?
31. What will your references tel us about you?
32. Tell me about a personal challenge you have faced.
33. What specific skills do you have that are required for this job?
34. Tell me a little about a situation
where you had a disagreement with a co-worker.
35. What is the biggest problem you have faced recently
and how did you handle it?
36. What part of this job is least attractive to you?
37. What part of this job appeals to you the most?
38. What are the hours of work you are looking for?
39. What would you like to achieve in this job?
40. Tell me about some of your accomplishments in a former job.
41. How would you describe your most recent job performance?
42. What kind of supervisor do you work best for?
43. How has your education/training helped you prepare for this position?
44. Do you prefer to work alone or as part of a team?
45. What could you do to "fit into" a new work environment?
46. What three personal traits best describe you?
47. What makes a good manager?
48. Why do you want this job?
49. What are some trends that you see in the future for our industry?
50. Describe what you think would be a typical day in this job.

Some thoughts on possible answers to 10 of the most frequently asked questions are provided on the next two pages.

10 COMMON INTERVIEW QUESTIONS AND ANSWER TIPS

As you answer each of the following, emphasize:
- the positive
- use specific examples to support what you are saying
  (remember, you have examples from activities
  throughout this book to support your answers)
- how the company would benefit from hiring you

1. Tell me about yourself . . .
   (see BOX 6 on page 33 and/or BOXES 7-10 on pages 37 + 38)
   Select 2-3 of your strengths that tie in with what the company is looking for. Be confident, but not arrogant. Stress how your strengths can help the company.

2. What are your strengths/weaknesses?
   (for your strengths, focus on the information you provided on pages 33, 37, and 38 of this book)
   Your strengths should be answered similar to #1 above. For your weaknesses, be honest, but avoid anything that makes you look bad in your relationship with others. If possible, choose a weakness that you are currently trying to resolve such as "My typing speed is 30 words per minute, but I am taking an evening course in keyboarding to help improve this."

3. Why do you want to work for us?
   This is an opportunity to show that you know something about the company. Present a positive impression of the company and show how your skills/training are a good match for the company (research the company on their website).

4. Why should we hire you?
   Talk about what you can do for the company in relationship to their needs.

5. Tell me about a conflict you had with a former co-worker or manager and how you handled it. (see the tips on page 24)
   Choose an example that has a positive resolution if possible. Stress that you handled this in private and attempted to understand the other person.

6. What are your short term/long term goals?

Your short term goal would be to make a positive contribution to the company as quickly as possible. Hopefully, five years from now you will have greater responsibilities allowing you to take on greater challenges within the company. Stress that you will be loyal to the company.

7. Describe your ideal boss.

Never belittle any former supervisor or manager. Select words such as fair, honest, good listener and optimistic to describe your ideal boss. Also mention that you would like to work with someone who is dedicated to the company and has a vision of where the company is going.

8. Describe a time when you worked on a team project.

Talk about how you believe that a team can be more effective than an individual completing a task. Emphasize cooperation, good listening skills and the need to support others.

9. Tell me about a time when you failed doing something.

Don't try to avoid this question. We all have our failures. Avoid examples that portray you in a bad manner in your relationship with others. Talk about growing and learning from your failures.

10. Describe one of your most important achievements.

(see pages 37 + 38 for possible examples)

Be specific. Tell the achievement as a story. Show how your achievement helped the company you worked for. Explain what you did and how others benefited from your accomplishment. Think about a time when you saved the company money or found a better way of doing something. If you are using a non-work example, stress how your achievement made you a better person or helped others.

TIPS ON HANDLING JOB INTERVIEW STRESS

1. It is normal and okay to feel some stress
when you are being interviewed for a job.

2. One of the best ways to reduce stress is
by being well prepared.

3. If you are asked a question that is difficult for you to answer,
attempt to stay calm, positive, smile, and simply do your best.
When you are asked difficult questions, the manner in which
you answer may be as important as your actual answer.

4. Make a positive first impression with a firm handshake,
smile, and good posture.

5. Make sure you arrive at least 15 minutes
before the interview. As you are waiting for your
interview, be positive with anyone you meet.

6. Use stress reduction strategies such as exercising
or breathing techniques to reduce stress on a
regular basis. Once you have developed stress reduction
habits you can use these techniques to
help you stay more relaxed during an interview.
In addition, remember that you can decide
whether a job interview is a horrible experience
or a wonderful opportunity. It is your choice!

7. Visualize success. In your mind, before the interview,
picture yourself creating a strong positive impression
and effectively answering the questions you are asked.

SOME THOUGHTS ON GOOD LUCK

*"Those who succeeded at anything and didn't
mention luck are kidding themselves."*
Larry King

*"I'm a great believer in luck,
and I find that the harder I work, the more I have of it."*
Thomas Jefferson

"Luck is when opportunity knocks and you answer."
Anonymous

"The day you decide to do it is your lucky day."
Japanese Proverb

*"Each misfortune you encounter
will carry in it the seed of tomorrow's good luck."*
Og Mandino

*"Opportunity is missed my most because
it is dressed in overalls and looks like work."*
Thomas Edison

"Luck is what happens when preparation meets opportunity."
Seneca

*"Our deepest fear is not that we are inadequate.
Our deepest fear is that we are powerful beyond measure."*
Marianne Williamson

*"The thing that is really hard, and really amazing,
is giving up on being perfect and beginning
the work of becoming yourself."*
Anna Quindlen

"There are no short cuts to any place worth going."
Beverly Sills

NOTES

NOTES

Other Books by Brian Harris

Amazon Bestselling Author

CHOOSING
YOUR CAREER

Brian Harris, B.A., M.Ed.

**A Self-Directed Guide to Help You Identify
Your Interests, Abilities and Values to Help You
Choose the Career That is Best for You**

ISBN 9781460930885

Other Books by Brian Harris

TIME MANAGEMENT

Including 471 Tips To Help You Have More Time For Yourself

Brian Harris

Amazon Bestselling Author

ISBN 9781501019616

Other Books by Brian Harris

Amazon Bestselling Author

MONEY MATTERS

Brian Harris

A Step-by-Step Guide to Help You Get Out of Debt
and Enjoy Having More Money

ISBN 9781791613112

About the Author

Brian Harris is an award-winning teacher/counselor and best-selling author. He has extensive experience working in high schools, colleges, universities, and career counseling centers. He has achieved the designation of International Professional Speaker. Brian has a wide range of experience in the field of career/educational planning with both students and adults.

Brian lives in Ontario, Canada, with his wife and two daughters. In addition to writing, Brian is a part-time lecturer in counseling at Queen's University. He is also an accomplished artist (www.bcharris.com).

Brian enjoys family trips and is an avid canoeist and scuba diver.

Additional information about Brian can be found at

www.cgscommunications.com